HOUSE OF LORDS   SE

REPORT FROM THE SELECT COMMITTEE ON CHINOOK ZD 576

Ordered to be printed 31 January 2002

PUBLISHED BY AUTHORITY OF THE HOUSE OF LORDS
LONDON – THE STATIONERY OFFICE LIMITED

£10·00

HL Paper 25(iii)

CONTENTS

Q and QQ refer to questions in oral evidence. The oral evidence taken by the Committee, and selected written evidence, is printed in HL Papers 25(i) and (ii). It is also available in full on www.parliament.uk. Evidence not published and not confidential is available for inspection in the House of Lords Record Office: telephone 020 7219 3074.

CHINOOK ZD 576

31 JANUARY 2002

By the Select Committee appointed to consider the justification for the finding of those reviewing the conclusions of the RAF Board of Inquiry that both pilots of the Chinook helicopter ZD 576 which crashed on the Mull of Kintyre on 2 June 1994 were negligent.

ORDERED TO REPORT

PART 1: SUMMARY

1. On 2 June 1994, an RAF Chinook Mark 2 helicopter, ZD 576, crashed on the Mull of Kintyre. All those on board the aircraft were killed in the crash and the aircraft sustained catastrophic damage.

2. RAF rules in force at the time provided that deceased aircrew could be found negligent only where there was absolutely no doubt whatsoever. The RAF investigating board concluded that the most probable cause of the accident was that the crew had selected an inappropriate rate of climb to overfly the Mull. However the investigating board made no finding of negligence on the part of the pilots; nor did the two station commanders who reviewed their findings. Nevertheless the two Air Marshals to whom the investigating board's report was submitted in turn concluded that the pilots were negligent in that they failed to take appropriate action when approaching deteriorating weather near the Mull. If they intended and were able to maintain visual flight they should have slowed down, turned away or turned back. If on the other hand they were forced by the presence of cloud to change from visual to instrument flight, they should have climbed to safety altitude at maximum power while turning away. It appeared to both the investigating board and the Air Marshals that the aircraft had flown straight towards the Mull without altering course for some 20 or more seconds before the crash.

3. The House of Lords appointed us, in July 2001, to consider whether this finding of negligence was justified. In preparing this report we have not only considered the evidence which was before the investigating board and hence the reviewing Air Marshals, but also additional evidence both oral and written. This additional evidence related among other things to the weather in the area at the time of the crash, to various mechanical problems which had affected Chinook Mk 2 helicopters since their introduction into RAF service, and to what reliance could be placed upon the results of a mathematical simulation carried out by the aircraft manufacturers, Boeing, to determine the movements of the aircraft during its last few seconds of flight.

4. Information extracted from the navigation equipment showed that, when the aircraft was 0.95 nm from the point of impact on a given bearing, a "way point change" was made to the navigation equipment to show the course and distance to Corran in Argyll, the next staging point on the intended route. There was no information as to the time this change was made, or the course and speed of the aircraft. The same equipment also produced an approximate height for the aircraft at an approximate number of seconds before impact, but neither position nor speed. A cockpit instrument showed a certain speed at impact. These results were much relied upon by the investigating board and the Air Marshals as demonstrating the final movements and speed of the aircraft.

5. From this information, and from certain other information as to the position of the aircraft and some of its components at impact, Boeing concluded that the aircraft had

made a final "flare"[1] upwards some 4 seconds before impact, and that for an unspecified time before this the aircraft was climbing at a rate of 1000 ft per minute at an airspeed of 150 knots, which with a tail wind of 25 knots gave a groundspeed of 175 knots or thereabouts.

6.   For reasons set out in our report, we consider that Boeing's conclusions cannot be relied upon as accurate. Since these conclusions are the basis for the conclusions of the investigating board and the Air Marshals that the aircraft was under control at the time of the final flare, it follows that there is insufficient evidence to the required standard of proof that this was the case.

7.   The additional evidence which we heard as to the weather came from a yachtsman who was sailing near the Mull at the time. He considered that when he saw the aircraft some 300 yards away the crew would have been able to see the land mass of the Mull. There was evidence before us from experienced helicopter pilots that, when a way point change is made to the navigation equipment, it is usual for pilots to change course towards the next way point at that time or shortly afterwards. In these circumstances we concluded that there could not be said to be absolutely no doubt whatsoever that the pilots intended to overfly the cloud-covered Mull; indeed the opposite is a distinct possibility if not more likely.

8.   We heard a good deal of evidence about mechanical problems suffered by Chinook Mk 2s. Some of these problems were intermittent, leaving no trace, and others were readily detectable. Although no trace of any mechanical fault, other than a defective radar altimeter, was found by the Air Accidents Investigation Branch inspector, he was unable to dismiss the possibility of an undemanded flight control movement, an engine run up or a control jam having occurred. Any of these events could have had a serious effect upon the crew's ability to control the aircraft. Once again we consider that it could not be said that there was absolutely no doubt whatsoever that some mechanical failure had not caused a loss of control of the aircraft.

9.   It is not our role to determine the likely cause of this accident, and indeed on the evidence which we have heard and read it would be impossible to do so. We are nevertheless satisfied, on the evidence before us and against the standard of "absolutely no doubt whatsoever", that the Air Marshals were not justified in finding that negligence on the part of the pilots of ZD 576 caused the crash.

---

[1]   A rapid change in pitch angle of the aircraft, either to slow down or to climb quickly.

PART 2: INTRODUCTION

THE CRASH

10. At about 17.59 hours on 2 June 1994 an RAF Chinook Mark 2 helicopter, ZD 576, on a flight from Aldergrove to Inverness, crashed into a cloud-covered hill on the west side of the Mull of Kintyre, a short distance inland of and uphill from the lighthouse. The pilots, Flight Lieutenants Jonathan Tapper and Richard Cook, the other two crewmen and the 25 passengers, who were all senior members of the Northern Ireland security services, were killed.

RAF BOARD OF INQUIRY

11. The RAF immediately convened a Board of Inquiry to investigate the accident, consisting of Wing Commander (now Group Captain) A D Pulford and two Squadron Leaders, one a pilot with experience of helicopters and the other an engineer. Its terms of reference included:

    "(a) Investigate the circumstances of the accident to Chinook HC2 ZD 576 at Mull of Kintyre on 2 June 1994.

    (b) Determine the cause or causes of the accident and examine related factors."

12. Wing Commander Pulford had never conducted a Board of Inquiry before (Q 5). It is perhaps surprising that an officer with no such experience should have been appointed to conduct an inquiry into an accident with such important and catastrophic consequences – an accident which was described to us by Air Chief Marshal Sir William Wratten as "the largest peace time tragedy that the Royal Air Force had suffered" (Q 437).

13. Board of Inquiry procedure is governed by rules[2] made under section 135 of the Air Force Act 1955 and by The Queen's Regulations for the RAF, chapter 17. The RAF Manual of Flight Safety AP 3207 published by the Inspectorate of Flight Safety and in force at the time of the accident provided in paragraph 9 of Annex G to Chapter 8 that *"only in cases in which there is absolutely no doubt whatsoever should deceased air crew be found negligent".*[3]

14. Paragraph 9 demanded a particularly high standard of proof, higher than is required of the prosecution in a criminal case in the United Kingdom ("beyond reasonable doubt"), and much higher than is required in civil litigation ("on the balance of probabilities"). It was no doubt set so high because deceased aircrew are no longer available to offer their own account of events. We consider that it requires all other plausible explanations for the crash to have been positively excluded. If any such explanations remain possibilities, the standard of proof has not been met. Furthermore, the fact that there is no evidence that an event giving rise to an explanation occurred will not amount to proof positive that it did not if such event could have occurred without leaving evidence of its occurrence or if evidence that it occurred could have been destroyed. Paragraph 9 is no longer in force; since 1997 RAF Boards of Inquiry have not been required or entitled to make findings of negligence.

15. The investigating board received evidence, oral and written, as well as a very detailed report from the Air Accidents Investigation Branch (AAIB). They concluded that the most probable cause of the accident was the selection of an inappropriate Rate of Climb (ROC) over the Mull. The investigating board did not find that either of the pilots was negligent. The investigating board delivered its report on 3 February 1995.

16. The next prescribed stage in the RAF Board of Inquiry process is review by the Station Commander. In accordance with the instructions of the Air Officer Commanding No.1

---

[2] Board of Inquiry (Air Force) Rules 1956 as amended.

[3] Annex G as in force at the time is printed in HL Paper 25(ii), p 81.

Group, Air Vice Marshal J R Day (as he then was, now Air Chief Marshal Sir John Day, Commander in Chief Headquarters Strike Command), the station commanders at both RAF Aldergrove and RAF Odiham commented on the findings of the investigating board. The former's remarks were brief. The latter, Group Captain P A Crawford, commented at some length. He disagreed with the investigating board as to an inappropriate ROC having been selected and concluded that the reasons for the accident were open to conjecture. He did not find that the pilots were negligent.

17. The final stages in the RAF Board of Inquiry process are review by the Air Officer Commanding and by the Air Officer Commanding-in-Chief. Air Vice Marshal Day himself accepted the preferred scenario of the investigating board, but concluded that both pilots were negligent to a gross degree. Air Chief Marshal Sir William Wratten, Commander in Chief Strike Command (now retired), agreed with Air Vice Marshal Day.

18. By kind and exceptional permission of the Secretary of State for Defence, at our request, the narrative report of the Board of Inquiry and the statement to the Board by the AAIB were placed in the public domain on 10 August 2001, and published by the House in November[4]. Other papers of the Board have been shown to us, but remain confidential.

FATAL ACCIDENT INQUIRY

19. In early 1996 there took place in the Sheriff Court Paisley a fatal accident inquiry (FAI) under the Fatal Accidents and Sudden Deaths Inquiry (Scotland) Act 1976. In terms of section 6(1)(b) of that Act, the Sheriff, Sir Stephen Young (now Sheriff Principal of Grampian Highlands and Islands), was required to make a determination setting out "the cause or causes of such death and any accident resulting in the death". Sir Stephen conducted an inquiry involving evidence and submissions over some 16 days, with representation as follows:

By counsel

The Crown

Ministry of Defence

Family of Flt Lt Tapper

Families of all deceased other than the pilots

Boeing Helicopters

By solicitor

Family of Flt Lt Cook

20. At the end of 123 pages of very detailed and careful analysis of the evidence[5], the Sheriff concluded,

> "it has not been established to my satisfaction, and on the balance of probabilities, that the cause of the accident was the decision by the crew of ZD 576 to overfly the Mull of Kintyre at cruising speed and their selection for that purpose of an inappropriate rate of climb. It may then be asked what was the cause of the accident. For my part I can only say that I do not know."

21. It will be noted that the Sheriff was applying the lower standard of proof in civil litigation as required by section 4(7) of the Act of 1976.

---

[4] HL Paper 25(i) 2001–02, published by TSO, ISBN 0 10 442022 7, £18.50. Full text on the Parliament website www.parliament.uk

[5] Published in full in HL Paper 25(ii).

22. The Ministry of Defence (MoD) have suggested[6] that the Sheriff's determination has little relevance to the present inquiry since the FAI had a different objective from the Board of Inquiry. However, section 6(1)(b) makes it clear that the cause of the relevant accident is a subject for his determination, as well as the cause of death. It is perfectly correct that it was not his duty to make a finding of negligence. But it was his duty to make a finding as to the facts which caused the accident. Negligence can only be inferred from facts and if the causative facts are not established there can be no negligence. Thus the Sheriff's inability to determine causative facts is entirely relevant because it means that no facts had emerged from which negligence could have been inferred.

HOUSE OF COMMONS DEFENCE COMMITTEE

23. The House of Commons Defence Committee produced a short report on the crash in May 1998[7]. They held only one hearing, with the Minister of State for the Armed Forces (Dr John Reid MP) and officials; they received a small amount of written evidence, including letters from Lord Chalfont and Mr Michael Tapper, the father of one of the deceased pilots.

24. The Committee did not offer its own view as to the cause of the crash.[8] Instead it considered some of the wider implications of the tragedy: the general performance and reliability of the Chinook Mk 2; Board of Inquiry procedure and the attribution of blame; training in movement between visual and instrument flight; black boxes, and the transport of special passengers. Its report concluded that "great sensitivity" is required in investigating fatal accidents in the armed forces; it acknowledged the efforts of Dr Reid in this regard. It also concluded that lessons learned from this case would help to avoid such controversies in the future.

25. Though the Defence Committee's report deliberately does not address the question set for us by the House, Dr Reid's testimony contains some highly relevant material. For instance, he enunciated clearly the MoD's position that the negligence of which the pilots were convicted consisted of "perceived failure ... to switch from visual flight rules to instrument flight rules ... as they approached bad weather"; and he went so far as to say that negligence "would have been deemed to have taken place had the crash not occurred" (Q 765). This proposition does not appear to us to have been advanced by either of the Air Marshals in his written remarks as reviewing officer.

26. Later, questioned by Menzies Campbell QC MP about the "absolutely no doubt whatsoever" standard of proof, Dr Reid acknowledged that it was "a very high burden of proof". He declined to be drawn into philosophical debate as to whether absolute certainty is ever achievable, offering instead the following test: "have we ruled out the possibility, on the basis of the evidence in front of us, that there was another possibility here?" (Q 917).

27. The Government responded to the report in October 1998.[9]

---

[6] E.g. in their response to the Commons Public Accounts Committee, para 30 – see fn 11 below.

[7] *Lessons of the Chinook crash on the Mull of Kintyre*, 4th report 1997–98, HC 611.

[8] "... we concluded that it would be helpful to clarify in a *public* forum some of the conflicting messages about the possible causes of the crash, and to put these into a wider context of concerns about the safety of the Chinook fleet. However, ... it was not our intention to become a further court of appeal, and **our inquiry and this report seeks neither to challenge nor endorse the findings of previous inquiries into the crash**" (para 3).

[9] Defence Committee 4th Report 1997–98, HC 1109.

HOUSE OF COMMONS PUBLIC ACCOUNTS COMMITTEE

28. The House of Commons Public Accounts Committee (PAC) reported in November 2000 on *Ministry of Defence: Acceptance of the Chinook Mk 2 helicopter*[10]. Unlike the Defence Committee, the PAC considered the verdict of the Board of Inquiry. They found it "unsustainable", and recommended that it should be set aside. They accused the MoD of "unwarrantable arrogance" in standing by it, particularly in the light of the inconclusive outcome of the Fatal Accident Inquiry, working as noted above to the lower standard of proof of "balance of probabilities".

29. The PAC took oral evidence from the National Audit Office, the Treasury, and officials from the MoD led by the Permanent Secretary. Written evidence included memoranda from Mr Malcolm Perks, an expert witness for MoD in a legal action in 1994–95 against the US firm which developed the Chinook Mk 2 Full Authority Digital Engine Control (FADEC) computerised fuel control system; and from the periodical *Computer Weekly*.

30. As the Committee charged with examining public spending, the PAC naturally took as its starting point the procurement of the upgrade which gave the RAF its Chinook Mk 2 fleet. It found this to have been flawed, particularly in respect of the software of the FADEC system. In 1994 the FADEC software was both faulty and "unverifiable": it defied independent evaluation by either the Aircraft and Armament Experimental Establishment (A&AEE) at Boscombe Down or EDS-SCICON, a firm specialising in testing software.

31. The PAC's doubts about FADEC led to its rejection of the finding of the Board of Inquiry, by two different routes. First, the Committee considered that a FADEC fault or other technical malfunction on ZD 576 was a real possibility, and that there was not enough evidence to rule this out, at least as a "potential" or "contributory" cause of the crash. In its view, "negligence should only be found where it can be positively identified to have been the cause of a crash ... it is impossible to prove gross negligence in the case of ZD 576". Second, it cast doubt on the "perceived objectivity" of the reviewing officers (though it did not impugn their integrity), on the grounds that they were "also responsible for the operational management of the Chinook fleet and minimising the disruption to support helicopter capability caused by the problematic introduction into service of the Mark 2".

32. The Government's response[11] rejected the Committee's conclusions. It denied that the FADEC software was poorly written and explained why Boscombe Down had had difficulty verifying it. It gave reasons why the Board ruled out a FADEC malfunction: both engines were running at the time of the crash, and the one digital engine control unit (DECU) which survived the impact had no trace of a fault or abnormality. It summarised the evidence underpinning the finding of negligence:

    - the weather;

    - the navigational information available to the pilots;

    - the fact that they had taken no avoiding action before or at the time of an action ("the way point change" – see para 53 below) taken 1.75km away from impact which seemed to indicate that the aircraft was under control;

    - the absence of evidence that the crash was due to technical malfunction.

33. The response declined to prefer the Sheriff's verdict to that of the Board. It insisted that the reviewing officers had met the high standard of proof required, and reached "an honest conclusion based upon the evidence" which would not be set aside without new

---

[10] 45th Report 1999–2000, HC 975.

[11] Treasury Minute on the 44th and 45th reports from the PAC 1999–2000, Cm 5078, March 2001.

evidence. It also insisted that "it is appropriate for the chain of command to be responsible for investigating accidents".

THE HOUSE OF LORDS INQUIRY

34. On 5 March 2001, shortly before the Government responded to the PAC, Lord Chalfont moved in the House of Lords "that ... the Liaison Committee[12] should consider the appointment of a Select Committee to consider all the circumstances surrounding the crash of Chinook helicopter ZD 576 on the Mull of Kintyre on 2 June 1994". The Government did not oppose this motion; indeed Baroness Symons of Vernham Dean, speaking as Minister of State at the MoD, appeared to give it some encouragement by observing that "the Air Marshals will then be able to explain properly in their own words to the Select Committee why they reached the conclusions that they did, something they have not been able to do properly before". The motion was agreed to without a division.

35. The Liaison Committee duly considered the matter, taking evidence from Baroness Symons and Lord Chalfont. By then the PAC had received the Government's response to their report, and it instructed its then Chairman, David Davis MP, to write to the Liaison Committee commenting on it in critical terms. This letter, and the other evidence, are printed with the Liaison Committee's report.[13]

36. The report dealt first with Lord Chalfont's proposal for a committee "to consider all the circumstances". It advised against this, on the grounds that it "would not be practical: it would take too long, and a House of Lords Committee would not be equipped to undertake it".

37. The Liaison Committee then considered the alternative proposal of a review limited to the justification for the decision of reviewing officers. Some members favoured this course. A majority, however, did not, for the following reasons:

   (a) To re-examine all the evidence would take a long time, and would still not put a Select Committee in a position to make a better judgment than experienced and senior professionals.

   (b) Whatever its conclusions, a Select Committee Report would be unlikely to put an end to the controversy.

   (c) Select Committees are a good vehicle for the examination of issues of public policy, but are not equipped to replicate the function of the higher courts in addressing alleged miscarriages of justice.

38. The Liaison Committee accordingly recommended against the appointment of a Select Committee. However, when on 30 April the Chairman of Committees invited the House to accept the report, Lord Chalfont moved the following amendment:

   "this House rejects the recommendations of the Liaison Committee and appoints a Select Committee of five members to consider the justification for the finding of those reviewing the conclusions of the RAF Board of Inquiry that both pilots of the Chinook helicopter ZD 576 which crashed on the Mull of Kintyre on 2 June 1994 were negligent".

39. The then Leader of the Liberal Democrat peers, Lord Rodgers of Quarry Bank, a member of the Liaison Committee at that time, had tabled an alternative to Lord Chalfont's amendment, in the form of a motion to resolve that

---

[12] One of the functions of the House of Lords Liaison Committee is "to consider requests for *ad hoc* committees".

[13] *Proposal for a Select Committee on the crash of Chinook helicopter ZD 576 on the Mull of Kintyre on 2 June 1994*, 2nd Report 2000–01, HL Paper 67.

"this House calls on Her Majesty's Government to set up an independent review of the conclusions of the Board of Inquiry into the crash of Chinook ZD 576 on the Mull of Kintyre on 2 June 1994".

40. For the Government, Baroness Symons indicated that Lord Rodgers' proposal was unacceptable, since the Government acknowledged no reason why they should expose the Board of Inquiry's judgment to review. She added that if the Liaison Committee were to reconsider the question and to recommend a committee along the lines now advocated by Lord Chalfont, the Government would not resist it. The Chairman of Committees indicated, however, that the Liaison Committee was highly unlikely to change its mind. The House therefore divided on Lord Chalfont's amendment, which was agreed to by 132 votes to 106.[14] Lord Rodgers' motion was not moved.

41. In short, the gestation of the Committee whose report this is was highly unusual. We are very conscious that a majority on the Liaison Committee, and a large minority of members of the House, believed that our Committee should not be set up at all. Set up we were, however, on 2 July 2001, and we have done our best to fulfil the remit given to us by the House.

---

[14] Of the members of this Committee, Lord Bowness and Lord Hooson voted for Lord Chalfont's amendment; Lord Brennan voted against it; Lord Jauncey of Tullichettle and Lord Tombs did not vote.

PART 3: FACTUAL BACKGROUND

INTRODUCTION OF CHINOOK MARK 2 INTO RAF SERVICE

42.   At the time of the accident ZD 576 had flown 66.5 hours since receiving the mid-life update (MLU) by the makers, Boeing, in the USA, which turned it from a Mark 1 into a Mark 2. The most significant part of this MLU was the installation of a Full Authority Digital Engine Control (FADEC) system. This consists of a number of components of which the two major ones are a digital engine control unit (DECU) and a hydro-mechanical assembly for each of the two engines. The purpose of FADEC is by control of the fuel supply to maintain approximately 100 per cent rotor speed in all conditions and to match engine torque between the two engines.

43.   FADEC had been fitted in a number of RAF Chinooks over the preceding years and had given rise to certain problems. In the summer of 1993 an independent defence IT contractor, EDS-SCICON, was instructed to review the FADEC software; after examining only 18 per cent of the code they found 486 anomalies and stopped the review. In October 1993 the Aeroplane and Armament Experimental Establishment (A&AEE) at Boscombe Down advised the MoD that because of the unverifiable nature of the FADEC software it could not recommend Controller Aircraft Release for the Chinook Mk 2. Both EDS-SCICON and A&AEE recommended that the FADEC software be rewritten but this was not done, and in November 1993 Chinook Mk 2s were released into operational service, subject to certain operational restrictions on the load which they could carry and the height at which they could fly thereby avoiding icing – restrictions which had not applied to the Chinook Mk 1. In addition intermittent engine failure captions were being regularly experienced by aircrew of Chinook Mk 2s and there were instances of uncommanded run up and run down of the engines and undemanded flight control movements (UFCMs).[15]

44.   On 1 June 1994 flying tests of the Chinook Mk 2 were suspended at Boscombe Down. Squadron Leader David Morgan, at that time Flight Commander of the Chinook Operational Conversion Unit, thought that this suspension was "connected with icing trials" and not due to FADEC difficulties (Q 484; cf MoD letter 2 Nov 2001, p 65 of HL Paper 25(ii)). However, in comments by the MoD[16] on a paper submitted to them by Lord Chalfont, it is stated:

> "Boscombe Down's decision not to authorise further trials flying in June 1994 was made against a background of several engine control system malfunctions that had occurred on the ground during start up checks, which had not at that point been explained to Boscombe Down's satisfaction by the aircraft or engine Design Authority. The necessary clarification was completed and accepted by Boscombe Down on 24 October 1994. Test flying was recommenced without any changes to the aircraft FADEC system, or any additional operating limitations. Operating flying continued within the weight restrictions applied."

45.   The MoD continued in relation to a memo of 3 June 1994 from Boscombe Down:

> "The 3 June 94 memo was an internal MoD working level document, the last sentence of which reads: "Notwithstanding the claims made in Textron's white paper, the problem remains that the product has been shown to be unverifiable and is therefore unsuitable for its purpose".

> But it is emphasised that this statement arose because Boscombe Down were unable to verify the software independently using their preferred analysis, which was neither mandated nor included in the development contract placed in 1985. Contractors had carried out their own validation and the fact that Boscombe Down

---

[15] See Board of Inquiry report part 2 para 35(d).

[16] 31 July 2001. Unpublished.

could not verify the software using their preferred software should not be taken to imply that there was an inherent problem with its design."

46.   A statement on behalf of the MoD to the FAI[17] included the following:

"As to the allegation that some pilots refused to fly the Chinook HC Mk 2 during CA Release trials at Boscombe Down, this is an over simplification of what actually happened and perhaps it would be helpful if some of the background was explained. On 7 March 1994 during one of the specified FADEC checks on the ground, the engine of an HC Mk 2 flamed out. Trials at Boscombe Down were halted while the failure was investigated. The failure was not due to a software fault and flying resumed on 20 April. However in the period up to 2 June 1994 there were a number of incidents involving airborne HC Mk 2 of which approximately 5 were due to FADEC malfunction whilst operating in normal mode. There had also been other incidents on the ground. The MoD(PE) Project Office sought explanations of the various incidents from the aircraft and engine manufacturers but in the absence of satisfactory explanations Boscombe Down suspended trials flying."

47.   It is clear from these quotations that at the time of the crash there were still unresolved problems in relation to the FADEC system of Chinook Mk 2s.

CIRCUMSTANCES OF THE ACCIDENT

48.   The aircraft took off from Aldergrove at 17.42 hours to fly to Fort George, near Inverness. The aircrew were members of the RAF Special Forces Flight and were all very experienced. The pilots were Flight Lieutenants Tapper and Cook of whom the former was captain and probably non-handling pilot. In the cabin were Master Air Loadmaster (MALM) Forbes and Sergeant Hardie. The former was considered to be an exceptionally professional crewman and entirely competent to check the navigation of the aircraft; indeed he had been observed on the preceding evening checking maps for this purpose. A four-man Special Forces crew work together as a unit more than in conventional flying, and it was the practice for one of the crewmen to act as second navigator.[18] After obtaining weather reports Flight Lieutenant Tapper decided that the flight to Fort George would be a low-level sortie flying under visual flight rules (VFR) and intimated that he was not intending to fly under instrument flight rules (IFR). Indeed flying under IFR in the vicinity of the mountains to the east of Ballachulish and Fort William would not have been permitted by the icing restrictions.[19] He therefore selected a route which included flying to the vicinity of the Mull of Kintyre lighthouse, which was programmed into the SuperTANS navigation system (see para 53 below) as way point (WP) A, and from there to Corran on Loch Linnhe, programmed as way point B.

49.   The aircraft was seen at Carnlough coasting out low over the Antrim coast towards the Mull of Kintyre. Shortly before 18.00 hours a yachtsman, Mr Mark Holbrook, who was some two miles south west of the lighthouse, saw the aircraft for some five seconds about 300 yards away. He estimated that its height was 200–400 feet and speed 60–80 knots, but he had never seen a Chinook before and was at the time involved in the

---

[17] See MoD letter 9 January 2002, p 86 of HL Paper 25(ii).

[18] Sheriff's determination pp 102-5 of HL Paper 25(ii); Q 789.

[19] Instrument flight must be conducted at or above a height ("safety altitude") 1000 ft above each of the high obstacles on the intended route (Q 280). Flt Lt Tapper had calculated the safety altitudes for the latter part of the sortie as 5900 ft Mull-Corran and 5800 ft Corran-Inverness. The CA Release precluded flight in an indicated temperature below +4 C. A weather aftercast shows that this temperature would have been reached at 5000 ft; and the Sheriff calculated that the crew may well have expected to reach it much lower, at 2500 ft (determination p 120 of HL Paper 25(ii)).

difficult operation of manoeuvring his vessel among a considerable number of trawlers which were fishing.

50. Mr Holbrook was the last person to see the helicopter. It was however heard immediately before and as it crashed by a number of witnesses at, and in the vicinity of, the lighthouse. The initial point of impact was 810 feet above mean sea level and about 500 metres east of the lighthouse, but the bulk of the aircraft remained airborne for a further 187 metres horizontally north and 90 feet vertically before coming to rest in pieces. Fire broke out immediately. All those on board sustained injuries from which they must have died almost instantaneously. The points of impact were shrouded in local cloud with visibility reduced to a few metres, which prevented those witnesses who had heard the aircraft from seeing it.

EXAMINATION OF WRECKAGE BY THE AIR ACCIDENTS INVESTIGATION BRANCH

51. On 3 June 1994 Mr Tony Cable, a Senior Inspector of the AAIB, flew to the crash site and remained closely involved thereafter in the investigation until he signed on 5 January 1995 the statement to the Board which he had prepared. This detailed report, which ran to some 66 pages and is published in HL Paper 25(i), resulted not only from Mr Cable's own work at the site and at AAIB Farnborough but also from opinions expressed by the relevant manufacturers to whom salvaged components or information had been provided.

52. The aircraft was very severely damaged: 80 per cent of the fuselage structure was appreciably damaged by ground fire, of which around 20 per cent was destroyed (AAIB statement para 7.1). It had neither cockpit voice recorder nor accident data recorder. This presented a formidable task to Mr Cable who expressed the view to us that "the evidence was remarkably thin" (QQ 956, 968, 1013). From the final position of the aircraft, which had by then extensively broken up, he estimated that at the initial impact the flight path was 20 degrees up relative to the horizontal, the pitch angle was 30 degrees nose up with a 5–10 degrees left roll and the ground speed was approximately 147 knots, as disclosed by detailed examination of the cockpit ground speed and drift indicator (AAIB statement para 6). The left rudder pedal appeared to have been applied 77 per cent (AAIB statement para 7.4.3, 7.4.9).

53. The aircraft was fitted with a Racal Avionics "SuperTANS" Tactical Area Navigation System providing navigation information from two independent sources. The system enables a number of way points to be fed into it before a flight. When flying from the point of departure to the first way point the screen[20] shows bearing, distance and "time to go" from the aircraft's current position to the way point. When the pilot alters the system from the first way point to the second, the distance and bearing of the former are replaced on the screen by those of the latter and so on as way points are progressively changed. Racal confirmed that the system was performing perfectly at the time of loss of power and extracted from its memory the information that way point B had been selected when way point A was 0.81 nautical miles distant, bearing 018°. The distance from the way point change to the point of impact was 0.95 nautical miles. The system gave no information as to height or time at the way point change but had recorded that at approximately 15–18 seconds before power down the aircraft was at a height of 468 feet ± 50 feet (Board report para 49). The manufacturers have told us that "18 seconds is likely to be a better estimate".[21] The TANS had also recorded that the height above sea level at impact was 665 ft[22], whereas in fact it was 810 ft. The investigating board noted

---

[20] Illustrated in slide 23 on p 134 of HL Paper 25(i).

[21] Note from Thales Avionics, 6 December 2001, unpublished for reasons of commercial confidentiality.

[22] Report by Racal Avionics (now Thales Avionics), Annex Y to the Board of Inquiry report. A restricted document, released to us in confidence by kind permission of Thales Avionics.

this discrepancy (para 49); they considered it probably due to "the mechanics of the crash and the developing fireball", but we know of no evidence to support this. The TANS is not intended to act as a Flight Recorder or what is colloquially known as a Black Box, and the information referred to above was achieved by a somewhat complicated and ingenious method of extraction employed by Racal.

54. The AAIB considered the engines and controls and because of the reported FADEC service difficulties investigated the DECUs in detail. DECU no. 2 remained partially functionable with deficiencies consistent with impact damage, and with no faults or exceedances traced in its memory of the last flight. DECU no. 1 had suffered gross fire damage with part of its casing melted away and severe damage to the interior components whereby its memories of exceedance and fault listing had been destroyed.

55. A detailed examination of the flight control mechanical linkages was carried out and the AAIB stated, "No evidence to suggest a control jam was found, although such a possibility could not be excluded, given the level of system damage" (para 7.4.2).

56. Important parts of the hydraulic flight control systems were housed in a small closet, colloquially known as the "broom cupboard", at the rear of the cockpit. There were two control pallets containing respectively 23 and 26 threaded inserts for component attachment. On 10 May 1994 the thrust balance spring attachment bracket on the aircraft's thrust/yaw control pallet had detached; this was due to the somewhat inadequate method of attaching the inserts to the pallet. This detachment had resulted in an undemanded flight control movement (UFCM) in the collective system.[23] An engineering report of the following day relating to this incident stated among other things,

> "Detachment of the bracket within the flying control closet during flight could present a serious flight safety hazard, with the danger of a detached bracket fouling adjacent flying controls".[24]

57. After the accident the investigators found that both inserts for the thrust balance spring attachment bracket had detached as well as most of the other inserts to both pallets. The AAIB stated, "as an insert could apparently pull out of the pallet without appreciable distress to the components necessarily resulting, the possibility that insert(s) had detached prior to the accident could not be dismissed" (para 7.4.2). In the Flight Control Summary the AAIB reiterated that "the possibility of control system jam could not be positively dismissed" and further stated that "little evidence was available to eliminate the possibility of pre-impact detachment of any of the pallet components" (para 7.4.9).

58. The investigators also found a considerable quantity of very small metallic particles and four fine metal slivers in the hydraulic system of the lower control actuators which form part of the flight control system. They concluded that this contamination had occurred pre-impact, but that it had not contributed to the accident (AAIB statement para 7.4.4).

59. With a view to ascertaining the manoeuvre necessary to produce the initial impact conditions the airframe manufacturers, Boeing, at the request of the Board produced mathematical models simulating the aircraft's final behaviour from a postulated range of initial steady flight conditions. In order to do this they were provided by Mr Cable with what he considered to be the pitch attitude and flight path angle of the aircraft at initial impact together with the extensions found in two components of the flight control system, namely, the differential airspeed hold (DASH) actuators and the longitudinal cyclic trim actuators (LCTAs), and other pieces of information derived from the site (Q 950 and p 86 of HL Paper 25(ii)).

---

[23] According to the investigating board's report, para 35(b)(3). In evidence to us, however, Gp Capt Pulford said that the effect would be to change "the feel of the controls" (Q 38).

[24] DHS follow-up report of serious occurrence or fault, signed by Gp Capt A M Verdon, HS31.

60. The Boeing simulation tried a series of input conditions suggested by AAIB, but found that close simultaneous matching of the predicted conditions with the control criteria was possible in only a few cases. A ready match was found where initial conditions combined an airspeed of 150 knots[25] with a rate of climb (ROC) of 1000 ft/min (AAIB statement para 8). In order to achieve a maximum ROC, which far exceeds 1000 ft/min, airspeed requires to be reduced to 80 knots or below. Boeing then estimated that, some four seconds before the initial impact, input was applied to the controls to achieve a "cyclic flare", increasing the ROC and decreasing forward speed by bringing the nose up.

61. At initial impact Boeing's simulation produced the following result (AAIB statement para 8):

Airspeed –	135 kt
Normal Acceleration –	2.2 g
Rotor Speed –	204 rpm (91%)
DASH Extension –	23%
LCTA Extension –	Virtually Fully Extended
Aircraft Pitch Attitude –	31° Nose Up
Aircraft Roll Attitude –	5° Left
Aircraft Yaw Attitude –	1° Left
Flight Path Angle –	20° above the horizontal
Climb Rate –	4670 ft/min
Horizontal Distance Travelled –	822 ft (250 m)
Vertical Distance Travelled –	128 ft
Groundspeed –	158 kt

[25] With a tailwind component of 24 knots, this would give a groundspeed of 174 knots.

PART 4: ANALYSIS OF FINDINGS AND CONCLUSIONS OF THE BOARD OF INQUIRY

EVIDENCE TO THE BOARD

62.   The Board heard the evidence of 22 witnesses and also had before it a considerable number of statements from witnesses taken by the Strathclyde Police and the Royal Ulster Constabulary. Most of the former related to weather conditions and events in the vicinity of the points of impact while the latter described the coasting out of the aircraft from Northern Ireland.

WEATHER

63.   The state of the weather was crucial to the conclusions of the investigating board and of the two Air Marshals. Two witnesses gave oral evidence to the Board as to weather. First Mr Murchie, a keeper at the lighthouse, spoke of visibility there being some 15–20 metres, but 400–500 metres to the north. The Board asked him no further questions about weather. The second was Mr Holbrook, the yachtsman, whose initial statement to the Strathclyde Police contained an expression of opinion "that the helicopter pilot would have been in a position to clearly see the local land mass". In his statement to the Board Mr Holbrook said that the aircraft was well below cloud level and visibility was about a mile limited by haze. At the time he was about two nautical miles south west of the lighthouse. He was asked three questions by the Board of which one was relevant to weather, namely whether he could see the physical features of the cliff on the Mull. To this he replied "no".

64.   When he gave evidence at the FAI Mr Holbrook expressed the opinion that the pilot could have seen "the location of the Mull lighthouse" and described the low cloud as "hugging the Mull" (Sheriff's determination, p 110 of HL Paper 25(ii)). He was criticised by the Ministry of Defence for having given different versions of his account to the Board and the FAI. In these circumstances we invited him to give evidence, an invitation which he willingly accepted.

65.   Mr Holbrook's evidence to us began with a statement which he had asked leave to make (Q 594). He explained that the low cloud clung to the contours of the high ground so that the location of the Mull massif itself was not in doubt from sea level. He considered that the crew of the aircraft when he saw it could determine without ambiguity where the Mull was and could see the cliffs, beach and lower perimeter walls of the lighthouse complex.

66.   Mr Holbrook reaffirmed that when he saw the aircraft he could not see the physical features of the Mull but he went on to explain that he was able to see the location of the lighthouse complex because the buildings and the white perimeter wall showed up as a colour change against the background of the land mass (QQ 594, 602). The top of the lighthouse was in cloud as the cloud level moved up and down (Q 606). Mr Holbrook went on to explain that the cloud was following the contours of the land and was very localised (Q 615). He also remarked, as he had done before the Board, that the helicopter was in sunlight as it passed (Q 619). At that time the aircraft was about two miles to the south west of the lighthouse. He expressed the opinion that the aircraft was flying at a height of between 200 and 400 ft and that the crew would have been better able to see the position of the lighthouse than he was at sea level with a certain amount of spray (QQ 610–13). He estimated the speed of the aircraft to be 60–80 knots but did not feel confident enough to be dogmatic as he had not previously seen a Chinook in flight. However, it was his impression that the aircraft was travelling sufficiently slowly to be involved in a search and rescue operation (Q 639).

67.   We do not consider that Mr Holbrook changed his evidence between his appearances before the Board and the FAI, rather that when he was subjected to professional examination and cross-examination at the FAI and to our questioning he was able to

expand upon the rather brief evidence which he had given to the Board. We had no hesitation in accepting him as a reliable and convincing witness.

68. In his statement to the police and in his evidence to us Mr Holbrook referred to the fact that the trawlers round which he was manoeuvring appeared to be Scottish as one of them had St Andrew's cross painted on the superstructure (Q 630). When Wing Commander (now Group Captain) Pulford gave evidence to us he was asked whether the Board sought evidence from any of the fishing vessels referred to by Mr Holbrook. He replied that they had tracked down the fishing vessels to Northern Ireland and the RUC could neither find anybody who had seen the aircraft nor trace some of the boats (Q 11).

69. It is perhaps surprising in view of Mr Holbrook's statement to the Strathclyde Police about the trawler with St Andrew's cross on the superstructure that that force were not asked to pursue the matter. It is perhaps even more surprising that the Board asked Mr Holbrook only one question in relation to weather and used the answer as a component in the construction of a theory as to the probable course adopted by the pilots.

70. Mr Holbrook explained to us that he had repeatedly but unsuccessfully asked to see photographs of a Chinook at different heights and ranges, in order the better to estimate the height and speed of the aircraft when he saw it. He clearly felt that he would have been in a better position to assist the Board had he been furnished with such information. We do not know why the Board did not accede to his request or afford him the opportunity of seeing a Chinook in flight.

71. The statements taken by Strathclyde Police which dealt with weather were all from persons on the Mull at or above the height of the lighthouse and did not therefore throw light on the extent to which the land mass could be seen from an aircraft approaching from seaward. These persons all spoke of being enveloped in cloud to a greater or lesser degree.

TECHNICAL MALFUNCTIONS

72. The investigating board referred to "unforeseen malfunctions" experienced by Chinook Mk 2s in RAF service, "mainly associated with the engine control system, including undemanded engine shut down, engine run up, spurious engine failure captions, and misleading and confusing cockpit indications". They found no evidence that any of these malfunctions had occurred on the aircraft's last flight. Their report however continued, "Nevertheless, an unforeseen technical malfunction of the type being experienced on the Chinook HC 2, which would not necessarily have left any physical evidence, remained a possibility, and could not be discounted" (para 35(d)). They went on to state that while technical failure was unlikely to have been the direct cause of the accident such a malfunction "could have provided a distraction to the crew". In our view a serious control jam or UFCM could provide the crew with a rather bigger problem than a mere distraction.

73. The board expressed the view that pre-impact detachment of an attachment bracket from the control pallets was "highly unlikely". They gave no reasons for thus going further than the conclusions of the AAIB (see above, para 57; and Mr Cable Q 1022).

74. The board's reference to the unforeseen malfunctions experienced by Chinook Mk 2s (see above) simply repeated the second half of an answer given by Squadron Leader Morgan to the following question by the board: "What unforeseen malfunctions have occurred on the Chinook HC2 since its introduction to service?" The first half of the answer was in the following terms: "The unforeseen malfunctions on the Chinook HC2 of a flight critical nature have mainly been associated with the engine control system FADEC." This answer was not followed up and indeed appears to be the only evidence relevant to previous malfunctions given by any of the witnesses before the board. Group Captain Pulford and Squadron Leader Cole, the engineering member of the

investigating board, were no doubt aware of the more general problems arising in Chinook Mk 2s at the time (QQ 64–5).

75. The board again referred to the fact that "the HC2 has experienced a number of unforeseen technical occurrences since its introduction into service", and said that the possibility of the crew being distracted by a technical fault, major or minor, which left no trace "could not be dismissed" and "could have been a contributory factor in the accident" (para 46(c)). However they rejected this as a probable cause.

CONCLUSION OF THE INVESTIGATING BOARD

76. After arriving at three scenarios unconnected with technical malfunctions, which could have been the cause of the accident, the investigating board concluded that the most probable was "the selection of an inappropriate rate of climb to overfly the Mull of Kintyre safely" (paras 59–60). In reaching this conclusion the board placed much reliance on the results of the Boeing simulation as to the final cyclic flare during the 4 seconds preceding the initial impact and the airspeed of 150 knots with a ROC of 1000 feet per minute prior thereto – a speed and ROC which have been shown to us to be incompatible (see below, paras 126–8). The board also considered that it was "most unlikely" that when the way point was changed the crew had seen the lighthouse or the Mull close to it (para 51).

77. In considering the position of the crew the board said, "although it is likely that Flight Lieutenant Tapper made an Error of Judgment in the conduct of the attempted climb over the Mull of Kintyre, it would be incorrect to criticise him for human failings based on the available evidence" (para 67(c)). The board concluded that "there were no human failings with respect to Flight Lieutenant Cook".

78. The board found no evidence that either MALM Forbes or Sergeant Hardie would have been in a position to affect the conduct of the flight as it approached the Mull (para 66). The board did not comment on the very close relationship which existed between each member of a Special Forces crew; the Sheriff went into this issue in some detail.[26] Nor did the board comment on the fact that MALM Forbes's body had been found in the forward fuselage section (AAIB statement para 5.11) – a position which suggests that he had been in the forward part of the cabin, probably by the right hand front door, where he would in all probability have been checking the navigation and therefore aware of the aircraft's course and proximity to land.

79. In view of the considerable number of problems which had beset Chinook Mk 2s since their entry into service – problems of which the investigating board appear to have been aware – it is perhaps surprising that they were able to dismiss so readily any such problems as having a significant effect in the accident.

REMARKS OF SENIOR OFFICERS ON THE INVESTIGATING BOARD'S FINDINGS

80. In his brief remarks the Station Commander at RAF Aldergrove, Group Captain R E Wedge, stated among other things,

> "I am impressed with the meticulous and detailed examination of events which the Board has provided. However, I believe that the exact train of events can never be determined with absolute certainty".

81. The Station Commander at RAF Odiham, Group Captain (now Air Commodore, retired) Peter Crawford, rejected the investigating board's conclusion that the most probable cause of the accident was selection of an inappropriate rate of climb. He explained that when approaching high ground in bad weather the appropriate action was ingrained in helicopter crews. They should (1) slow down and if necessary stop, (2) turn

---

[26] Determination pp 102–5 of HL Paper 25(ii).

away from high ground and if necessary turn back, and (3) if a climb was required do so on a safe heading at full power at the maximum rate of climb to at least safety altitude.

82. He went on to express the belief that the crew had seen the Mull, which prompted them to make the way point change, and had intended to follow the western coast of the Mull. His cogent argument for that belief was stated in these terms:

> "This WP change is crucial in trying to understand what the crew intended to do. If they had intended to abort at this stage and climb over the Mull despite the difficulty, which would have been so obvious to them, of clearing the high ground they would not have selected the Corran WP. Firstly, it removed from them the only easily interpretable information about the location of the high ground. Secondly, it was of little practical value; the crew would not have been able to climb to SA on track to Corran, in the hope of reverting to low level VFR, because of the forecast level of the 4°C isotherm. If they intended to climb over the Mull the only sensible option would have been to keep the lighthouse WP on until well clear of it and then to select the chosen diversion airfield. On the other hand, selection of the Corran WP was entirely appropriate if the intention was to follow the western coast of the Mull Peninsula and regain the planned track at the first convenient opportunity. In arriving at this alternative scenario I am now faced with the same problem that faced the Board – how did the aircraft get to around 500 ft, at 150 kts IAS with a ROC of approximately 1,000 ft per minute, which are the computed starting parameters of the final 18 seconds of flight?"

83. The Group Captain later in his remarks referred to the fact that at the time of the accident spurious engine fail captions lasting an average of 7–8 seconds were an increasingly frequent occurrence and were not well understood. In his conclusions he stated that the reason why the crew flew the aircraft into the ground was "open to conjecture" and that in the absence of firm evidence there was not much to be gained by "speculating on the actions that led to the last few seconds of flight", although he expressed the opinion that the aircraft was under control when it was flared shortly before impact – an opinion based apparently on the Boeing simulation. He stated that "there is sufficient evidence to conclude that ... there was no major technical failure that would have an implication for the Chinook fleet". In evidence before us he accepted that this was a matter of judgment on his part (Q 884). He expressed the view that, while there might arguably be some mitigating circumstances, Flight Lieutenant Tapper as captain of the aircraft had failed in "his overriding duty to ensure the safety of the aircraft". This did not amount to a finding of negligence (Q 902).

84. The Air Officer Commanding No.1 Group, Air Vice Marshal J R Day (now Air Chief Marshal Sir John Day), remarked that "when the aircraft crashed, it was flying at high speed, well below Safety Altitude in cloud (in Instrument Meteorological Conditions) in direct contravention of the rules for flight under either Visual Flight Rules [VFR] or Instrument Flight Rules [IFR]". He further stated,

> "On approaching the deteriorating weather near the Mull, they had two choices. If they intended and were able to maintain flight under Visual Flight Rules, they should have slowed down, turned away or turned back. If they planned to continue their flight under Instrument Flight Rules, they should have climbed to above Safety Altitude well before they approached the Mull. If they were forced to transition to Instrument Flight Rules because they inadvertently entered cloud when close to the Mull, they should have made a rapid climb to at least Safety Altitude at maximum power and best climbing speed, while also turning away from the Mull."

85. The Air Vice Marshal concluded that both pilots were "negligent to a gross degree". He commented that it was "incomprehensible why two trusted, experienced and skilled pilots should ... have flown a serviceable aircraft into cloud covered high ground".

86. The Air Officer Commanding in Chief Strike Command, Air Chief Marshal Sir William Wratten, remarked,

> "Lamentably, all the evidence points towards them having ignored one of the most basic tenets of airmanship, which is never to attempt to fly visually below safety altitude unless the weather conditions are unambiguously suitable for operating under Visual Flight Rules."

87. Therefore he agreed with the summary and verdict of the Air Vice Marshal. Neither of the Air Marshals referred to the change of way point shortly before the accident, nor commented on Group Captain Crawford's reasoning in relation to it. Both Air Marshals at this stage appear to have proceeded on the basis that

(a) the pilots never saw the Mull,

(b) no technical failure or malfunction occurred which deprived the pilots of control up to the point of impact, and

(c) the Boeing simulation provided a reasonably accurate demonstration of the aircraft's movements for a period prior to impact.

PART 5: EVIDENCE BEFORE THIS COMMITTEE

WITNESSES

88. In addition to Mr Holbrook we heard the evidence of:

- Group Captain Pulford, the president of the investigating board,

- Air Chief Marshals Sir John Day and Sir William Wratten,

- Air Commodore Crawford,

- Squadron Leader Morgan,

- Mr Cable and two colleagues from the AAIB,

- three fellows of the Royal Aeronautical Society, Captains Ron Macdonald, Richard Hadlow and Ralph Kohn, who had prepared a report on the crash,

- Squadron Leader Robert Burke, who was at the time of the crash the maintenance test pilot at RAF Odiham, but is now retired,

- Witness A, a very experienced and highly decorated Special Forces Chinook pilot who was at the time based at Odiham, and

- Mr Michael Tapper and Captain John Cook, the fathers of the two deceased pilots.

89. We also received a considerable number of documents from the MoD and many others which were intended to assist or influence us in our deliberations. We are grateful to all these persons for their assistance; they are listed in Appendix 2.

90. The Secretary of State for Defence, the Rt Hon Geoffrey Hoon MP, kindly offered to give evidence himself to us on the position of the MoD[27]. We decided not to trouble him, since he was not in office at the time of the crash and the Board of Inquiry, and since the question before us concerned a decision reached by others at that time rather than any aspect of current policy. We record our appreciation however for the full and helpful co-operation of staff at all levels in the Royal Air Force and the Air Secretariat of the Ministry of Defence. At a time when other serious matters demanded their attention, they responded promptly to our many queries and requests. In particular they arranged for us to fly to the Mull in a Chinook on 25 September, and for one of our number to inspect a partially dismantled Chinook at RAF Odiham on 22 October.

91. What follows is not an exhaustive summary of the evidence, but a considered analysis of those elements on which we base our conclusions.

WRITTEN EVIDENCE OF MR MALCOLM PERKS

92. In addition to the detachment of the balance spring on 10 May 1994 the aircraft had experienced some other problems in the weeks prior to the accident. On 21 April 1994 a torque mismatch occurred which lasted for about 1 second before returning to normal. No fault codes were indicated on the DECUs. On 17 May 1994 number one engine power caption came on and engine temperature reached 950 degrees. The engine was thereafter rejected due to overheating but on inspection nothing suspect was found. On 26 May 1994 number two engine failed caption came on spuriously and went out after 10 seconds.

93. In 1989 a Chinook HC2 engine owned by the MoD was destroyed on test at Wilmington, Delaware, USA as a result of a runaway[28]. The MoD initiated claims against Textron-Lycoming the manufacturers of the engine and Boeing who were

---

[27] See p 84 of HL Paper 25(ii).

[28] An engine "runaway" is an engine run up which is not controlled.

responsible for the test. Boeing settled but the case against Textron-Lycoming went to arbitration later and resulted in a substantial award in favour of the MoD. The claim against Boeing rested solely on negligence in carrying out the test whereas that against Textron-Lycoming proceeded on the basis that they had failed to exercise due care in the design, development and test of the FADEC system.

94. Mr Malcolm Perks, who now lives in Canada and who had spent many years working in the field of FADEC, provided technical evidence to the arbitration on behalf of the MoD. He was invited to assist us and accepted the invitation by furnishing two memoranda (p 87 of HL Paper 25(ii)). Although it has been repeatedly maintained on behalf of the MoD that the problem at Wilmington was due entirely to negligent testing Mr Perks suggested to us that if that had been the case it would have been unlikely that, Boeing having settled, Textron-Lycoming would also have been found negligent in respect of testing alone without any liability for design or development. Mr Perks had not seen the reasons for the finding of the arbitration board and nor have we.

95. The FADEC system incorporates fault codes in its memory so that maintenance staff can see what has happened and correct the fault. The fault condition implied by the E5 fault code was heavily implicated in the incident at Wilmington and the same fault code was found in the surviving DECU after the crash of ZD 576 (AAIB statement para 7.3.2.4). There has been much speculation that the coincidence of the E5 faults pointed to a runaway engine in ZD 576 as at Wilmington.

96. Mr Perks in his memoranda explained to us that the Wilmington incident was not caused by an E5 fault alone but by its conjunction with another fault and that by 1994 because of the action of the system designers an E5 fault was being dismissed as a nuisance fault of no significance. Furthermore Mr Cable explained that the DECU had two portions to the memory of faults namely (i) retained faults since its last overhaul and (ii) faults since the last engine start. The E5 fault in ZD 576's DECU was found in the former historical portion and not in that of the last flight. In all these circumstances we are satisfied that an E5 fault had no relevance to the accident.

97. The FADEC system used in Chinook Mk 2s has a built-in protection to prevent destructive overspeed resulting from a runaway engine. Mr Perks explained that, even if the runaway was contained within the engine's speed limits, it could cause major controllability issues due to rapid acceleration of the rotor system.

EVIDENCE OF MR CABLE, AAIB

98. As already mentioned, Mr Cable in evidence to us stressed that throughout the investigation the evidence was "remarkably thin" (QQ 956, 968, 1013). While the evidence available to him pointed strongly to the engines operating normally, i.e. without distress, at the point of initial impact, he conceded that this did not necessarily mean that this was in accordance with pilot commands (QQ 181–4). He further explained that the possibility of an intermittent fault prior to impact could not be dismissed (Q 182).

99. He further explained that the detachment of the pallet inserts and the components carried by them could possibly cause a restriction or jam. "It would be very difficult – impossible – to dismiss the possibility that there had been a restriction and evidence had not been found" (Q 196). This explanation is readily understandable given the crowded equipment in the broom cupboard. A balance spring is some 6 inches long by 1½ inches in diameter and its mounting bracket about 1½ inches long.

100. The only positive evidence of a fault possibly contributing to the accident was a radar altimeter system fault (AAIB statement para 7.2.17 and conclusions 48–9 and 52). However, in the light of all the evidence before us, we do not consider that this fault is likely to have been relevant.

101. Mr Cable summed the situation up thus:

   "Where there is no fault found that does not mean that there was not a fault present. In this case I found it probable that on the engineering side as far as I could see there was not a fault highly relevant to the accident, but I certainly could not dismiss that possibility" (Q 264).

102. As already referred to in paragraph 58, the AAIB investigation disclosed a considerable quantity of very small metallic particles in residual hydraulic fluid in parts of the boost actuator for both the pitch integrated lower control actuator (ILCA) and the thrust lower control actuators (LCAs) together with the presence of four fine metal slivers up to 0.2 inches long on one of the servo valve screens of the yaw ILCA boost actuator. This contamination was thought to have been present prior to the accident (AAIB statement para 7.4.4).

103. In evidence Mr Cable expressed the opinion that a failure of both lower control actuator systems due to hydraulic contamination would be unlikely to be a major problem as it would merely reduce the boost on the pilot's control to the upper boost actuators which drive the rotor blades[29]. A jam of an upper boost actuator would be a very different matter (QQ 204–10).

104. The US Army, however, who operate very large numbers of Chinooks, take a different view. In a report of June 1997[30] on an incident when a Chinook turned upside down at about 1100 feet and righted itself at about 250 and where no exact cause could be established, hydraulic contamination was considered to be a possible cause. The recommendations section of the report[31] referred to "uncommanded oscillations, flight control movements, and flight attitude changes" possibly related to the performance of the upper boost actuators and metal contamination in part thereof.

105. The recommendations continued,

   "An additional critical area is the integrated lower control actuators (ILCA). The metal contamination and moisture found in the pitch, roll and yaw ILCAs are considered critical to FLIGHT SAFETY. The amount of contamination found in the pitch and roll ILCA were considered sufficient to cause a disturbance in the normal operation of these components at any time. One solution may be to establish a drain point for each system 2 ILCA, since the corrosion and moisture contamination appears to be primarily found in system 2. CCAD shop personnel reported that some ILCAs arrive with secondary valves jammed due to internal corrosion. This means the unit is operating on the primary control valve with no back-up or secondary valve available. If the primary valve jams, in this situation, the capability to direct hydraulic fluid flow ceases.

   The upper boost actuators and ILCAs deserve immediate and positive action, since these two areas are CRITICAL TO FLIGHT SAFETY, PERSONNEL SAFETY, AND EQUIPMENT SAFETY."[32]

EVIDENCE OF SQUADRON LEADER DAVID MORGAN

106. Squadron Leader Morgan (QQ 473–86) referred to the over-speed check in the FADEC system which prevented an engine running up and thereby damaging or losing the rotor system. Boscombe Down had insisted that this mechanism be checked before each flight because of "a number of unresolved issues" with FADEC. During such checks

---

[29] Mr Cable compared the effect to losing the power steering in a car.

[30] By Corpus Christi Army Depot Analytical Investigation Division, ref SIOCC-QP-AI USASC 97-305.

[31] Reproduced on p 69 of HL Paper 25(ii).

[32] Emphasis original.

engines overheated and sometimes ran up (cf Burke Q 677). He had no personal experience of a run up nor of any flight-critical malfunctions but was aware of spurious engine failure captions in the control instruments which were capable of providing a distraction of up to 10 seconds depending upon circumstances. He explained that an engine run up which increased rotor RPM would increase vibration levels and render more difficult the reading of instruments (QQ 546–7).

EVIDENCE OF SQUADRON LEADER ROBERT BURKE

107. Squadron Leader Burke had extensive experience in flying helicopters including Chinooks Mks 1 and 2 and was described by his unit commander in April 1993 as having air-testing skills on the Puma and Chinook which were unique. He was able to provide us with useful information about the problems which he had experienced when testing Chinooks. At the outset of the investigation into the accident he was contacted by Mr Cable and had two or three telephone discussions with him in relation to control positions (QQ 658, 662). Thereafter he had nothing further to do with the Board of Inquiry.

108. After Squadron Leader Burke gave evidence, Group Captain Pulford submitted a statement to us (p 68 of HL Paper 25(ii)) in which he sought to explain why Squadron Leader Burke had not been asked to give evidence to the investigating board. He stated that as the Chinook maintenance test pilot "his flying was conducted in accordance with limited and pre-determined flight test schedules and he therefore lacked the operational currency to provide relevant evidence to the inquiry". This reasoning seems to assume that problems which Squadron Leader Burke might have encountered on test would not or could not occur in operational flying – an assumption whose justification we feel to be in doubt.

109. Squadron Leader Burke spoke to having experienced two engine run ups on the ground at the Boeing factory in Philadelphia while flying with an American Army test pilot (Q 655) and similar run ups when testing the overspeed limiter on the ground at Odiham (Q 680). He also spoke to problems with the multi-point connectors which went from the engines into the DECU. These were of bad design and liable to be displaced by vibration which then produced a power interruption. Although there was a back-up system this did not always work and on two or three occasions pilots had lost control of the engine condition lever. As a result squadrons introduced a procedure whereby crewmen every quarter of an hour checked that the connections had not been displaced in flight (QQ 677–9).

110. At the time of the accident DECUs still presented recurring problems. They were removed from the aircraft when something had gone wrong and returned to the makers who on many occasions could find no fault (QQ 698–9).

111. In relation to possible jams Squadron Leader Burke explained that, due to the complexity of the Chinook control system, a jam caused by a loose article such as the balance spring in the broom cupboard in one of the three axes, pitch, yaw or roll, could lead to quite random results in all three axes sometimes and certainly in two of them. He had personal experience while lifting off from the ground of a jam in one axis affecting the other two (Q 935). He also referred to the problems of DASH runaways in Chinooks of both marks causing temporary loss of control of aircraft (Q 929).

112. Finally, Squadron Leader Burke commented on the rudder input of 77 per cent left yaw found in the wreck of ZD 576:

"That is an enormous rudder input. It is unthinkable to put that in at high speed. As I may have explained, particularly in the Chinook but in any helicopter, the helicopter does not use the yaw input for control once you have gone over 20 knots. It puts an enormous strain on the aircraft because you obtain yawing control in the simplest way by tilting the rotors one left, one right. You are spinning the aircraft about its middle. It is quite difficult to do. The rudder is quite heavy on a

Chinook. You have to make a real effort to put that amount of control in. The only conceivable reason that I can think of for putting that voluntarily in as a pilot is if you have partially lost control coming out and you are trying to counteract a yaw one way or the other" (Q 719).

113. Mr Cable told us that, though it was possible that this rudder input was applied before impact, it was also possible that it was due to the force of the impact itself (Q 999).

EVIDENCE OF WITNESS A

114. Witness A, who was a member of the Special Forces Flight with considerable experience of flying Chinooks operationally, had, at the time of the accident, experienced intermittent engine fail captions on a reasonably regular basis. He had subsequently experienced torque mismatches on an intermittent basis (Q 784). Pilots were instructed that if the failed captions remained on for more than 12 seconds they were to be treated as though something was wrong with the engine but if they stayed on for less than that time they could be ignored. When a caption came on in flight one of the crew was directed to check engine instrumentation and the engine itself (Q 786).

115. Witness A also had personal experience of UFCMs in Chinook Mk 1s (QQ 792–6). In one case over a period of days an aircraft bounced vertically every time it was turned right. Repeated unsuccessful attempts were made to find the cause and the problem eventually disappeared of its own accord. In another case in daylight the lights came on to maximum intensity, dimmed to minimum and the hydraulic gauges cycled between zero and maximum. The pilot reported that the aircraft was becoming difficult to control and Witness A ordered him to land at the first available opportunity. The subsequent engineering investigation found no fault.

116. Witness A, like Air Commodore Crawford, expressed cogent reasons for thinking that the crew of ZD 576 could see the land mass when they changed the way point and that this change was entirely consistent with a continued VFR flight to Corran on the new course (QQ 797–8). When asked whether he could think of any reason why having changed way point the aircraft should have continued on its existing course he replied, "That is the crux of the matter. I cannot think of any reason why the crew would have elected to do that unless they were not doing it of their own volition" (Q 802). He found it very difficult to accept that the crew were unaware of the proximity of the Mull (Q 804).

117. In answer to a question as to how much the unforeseen malfunctions occurring in the Chinook Mk 2 since its introduction were a matter of discussion among helicopter pilots, he answered,

"They occupied our minds to a great degree, crew room talk was of little else at the time. The crews felt extremely uneasy about the way the aircraft had been introduced into service. This perception was reinforced by the lack of information contained in the aircrew manual, the poor state of repair of the flight reference cards and such like as well" (Q 852).

118. It is interesting to note that the father of Flight Lieutenant Cook told us that, a few days before the crash, his son had expressed to him the view that neither his crew nor ZD 576 was yet ready to go on operations in Northern Ireland (Q 446).

119. We found Witness A an impressive witness, who plainly felt it his duty to assist us as he had assisted the Sheriff.

EVIDENCE BEARING ON THE BOEING SIMULATION

120. Since the investigating board and the Air Marshals placed considerable reliance on the Boeing simulation it may be convenient to refer to it again in more detail at this stage. Before doing so however it is necessary to examine the functions of the two major controls in the aircraft. The *collective* increases or decreases the pitch of all the blades

of the rotors as it is raised or lowered thereby causing the aircraft to climb or descend. At the same time movement of this control by connection to the FADEC system increases or decreases engine power to maintain rotor speed at approximately 100 per cent. The *cyclic stick* alters the pitch of the rotor head which is then tilted in the direction in which the aircraft is intended to go, namely forward, sideways or backwards.

121. Detailed examination by the AAIB of the flight control system disclosed that the DASH extensions found did not correspond to a high speed level flight condition whereas the · LCTA extensions did, and it appeared possible that the settings could reflect a dynamic aircraft manoeuvre at the point of impact. Boeing were therefore asked to undertake a study to assess the consistency of the settings and to define the possible manoeuvre. The simulation was a mathematical exercise which, as Mr Cable stated, was "looking really for fairly gross manoeuvres over a pretty short period of time" (Q 957). It was not intended to produce an accurate reconstruction of events but rather to demonstrate what could have happened within certain parameters (Q 982).

122. Mr Cable provided Boeing with his findings from the wreckage of the aircraft as to pitch attitude, flight path angle, actuator extensions and ground speed together with certain other information provided by the board (Q 950). Information from the SuperTANS disclosed that:

    (i)   When the way point change was made the aircraft was 0.81 nautical miles from way point A (0.95 nm from where it crashed), on a bearing of 018 degrees T to way point A (022 degrees T to where it crashed). No information as to height, speed or course was available; but, on the assumption of a straight course at a steady 150 knots, Racal (manufacturer of SuperTANS) suggested that this change was made "about 20 seconds before the accident".[33]

    (ii) Some 15–18 seconds before impact the aircraft was at a height of 458 plus or minus 50 feet at an unknown position, on an unknown course and at an unknown speed.[34]

123. The Boeing simulation considered a wide range of possible starting conditions, i.e. conditions pertaining immediately prior to a final manoeuvre. Having rejected possible conditions at an airspeed of 135 knots, they concluded that an airspeed of 150 knots (groundspeed 174 knots) with a ROC of 1000 feet per minute provided "a ready match" with the criteria and was therefore the most likely (AAIB statement para 8). From this simulation, using among other things the state of the actuator extensions and attitude of the aircraft as found by Mr Cable, Boeing deduced that 2.9 seconds after the final manoeuvre had been initiated[35] the airspeed was about 135 knots, the rotor speed 204 rpm or 91 per cent design speed and the groundspeed 158 knots.

124. It will be noted that, apart from the evidence of Mr Holbrook, there was no other evidence of the speed of the aircraft prior to the moment of impact. In the absence of a time at which the way point change took place and a position at which the height of the aircraft was disclosed, there are no facts from which the speed of the aircraft prior to the initiation of any final manoeuvre could be calculated. It follows that Boeing's 150 knots airspeed is a postulated figure rather than one calculated from known facts. This postulated figure then becomes the basis for the further postulated figure for ROC. Furthermore, the simulation gives no indication of the length of time prior to the assumed final manoeuvre during which the aircraft had been proceeding at the postulated airspeed.

---

[33] Report by Racal Avionics. See footnote 22.

[34] Investigating board report para 49.

[35] Mr Cable told us, "The manoeuvre started at the one second point from an arbitrary zero" (Q 987). Hence the Air Marshals' description of the final manoeuvre as lasting 4 seconds (eg QQ 280, 304).

125. The rotor speed of 91 per cent derived from the simulation is significantly different from that of 100.5 per cent found by the AAIB on the instrument panel (statement para 7.2.2). Maintenance of rotor speed at or about 100 per cent design speed is of critical importance for safe helicopter flying. If rotor speed falls much below 90 per cent there is a danger of the blades of each rotor coning up and meeting at the top due to the reduction in centrifugal force which at higher speeds keeps them apart (Q 918). FADEC is designed to keep rotor speed at normal design speed and, if rotor speed had fallen to 91 per cent, maximum if not emergency power from the engines would have been expected. The position of the DASH actuators was not consistent with the use of such power. Mr Cable doubted whether the 91 per cent figure was accurate (Q 971) but he also explained how difficult it was to know the time to which the 100.5 per cent reading on the instrument panel related given the fact that there were at least three different impacts before the aircraft came to rest (Q 967).

126. The groundspeed of 158 knots at impact derived from the Boeing simulation exceeded by 11 knots that of 147 found in the cockpit ground speed indicator (AAIB statement para 6). Moreover, the postulated ROC of 1000 feet per minute at 150 knots airspeed is unattainable. Squadron Leader Burke doubted whether it was achievable with ZD 576's load (Q 920). Witness A explained that while flying he had tried to see whether Boeing's chosen ROC was obtainable at 150 knots and had found that it was impossible in similar conditions (QQ 813–23). He had achieved no more than 400 feet per minute at 150 knots.

127. Sir John Day had arranged for someone to fly the Chinook simulator at 150 knots; they achieved a ROC of 650 feet per minute (Q 1075). He accepted that a ROC of 1000 feet per minute and a speed of 150 knots were not compatible (Q 1075). However, he put it to us that he had always said that the ROC was *about* 1000 feet per minute, not precisely that. This comment was made in the context of his own calculations, based on the range of heights shown by the TANS some 15–18 seconds before impact, which showed that between those times and the start of the final flare the range of possible ROC was between 650 and 1350 feet per minute. The simulator which produced a ROC of 650 feet per minute at 150 knots also produced one of 1150 feet per minute at 135 knots, which was a speed for which Boeing found it "very difficult or impossible" to match the predicted conditions with the initial impact data (AAIB statement para 8, QQ 1074–80).

128. The Boeing simulation postulations of a ROC of 1000 feet per minute and a speed of 150 knots were essential to the conclusion that a final flare was initiated some 4 seconds before impact. Now that those postulations have been shown to be unattainable, the circumstances and indeed existence of any such flare must be very doubtful. That there was such a flare was crucial to the Air Marshals' conclusion that the crew must have been in control of the aircraft for the last 4 seconds before impact (e.g. QQ 280, 1088). Sir John's calculations (above) give no support to such a conclusion, since they are independent of and in no sense a substitute for Boeing's postulations.

129. Furthermore Mr Cable explained that the Boeing simulation did not model FADEC. "It had to be a representation of a simple engine governor for each engine, which would have really quite different characteristics, I think, in small areas anyway, from the FADEC" (Q 957). The simulation presupposed that the aircraft was at all times under control and flying a straight course although there was no evidence that this was necessarily the case.

130. Mr Perks, who had worked on such simulations with a MoD team in the late 1970s and early 1980s, explained that for a given transient manoeuvre all the key modelled parameters had to be matched within reason to actual historical records. Two of the most important parameters were rotor speed and torque from the engines, in relation to which no historical records were available. He remarked on the disparity between the rotor speed required for the simulation and that indicated on the rotor speed gauge; and

also on the fact that, whereas the simulation manoeuvre required engine power to be at absolute maximum, the indications found by the AAIB were that the engines were at an intermediate power setting (Q 183). Furthermore, none of the witnesses on the Mull who had heard the aircraft had noticed any noise suggesting a violent manoeuvre, and there were no data to suggest that the engines had exceeded normal values.

131. Mr Perks proceeded,

"On the Chinook Mk 2 aircraft the engine control systems have aircraft rotor speed as a primary input, with collective pitch as a supplementary input. If the rotor speed is too high, the engine is driven to idle power. If too low, the engine is driven to maximum output power. If collective pitch is changed, the engines will also be affected. Any form of extreme manoeuvring would have forced the engine control systems to respond immediately. The engine controls should, therefore, have been anywhere other than at normal settings. Normal settings implies the engine controls were not seeing major changes in their inputs, and that is not consistent with the violent manoeuvring postulated by Boeing. Whatever the pilots were doing, collective pitch was not being affected, and neither was rotor speed, given the evidence in the wreckage."

Thereafter he expressed the belief that the simulation should be "discounted" as evidence.

132. Where does this leave the simulation? We conclude that it would be quite inappropriate to treat the results of the simulation as proven fact.

EVIDENCE OF THE AIR MARSHALS

133. Sir John Day began his evidence before us with an interesting and helpful presentation involving 34 slides which are reproduced in HL Paper 25(i). He explained that the VFR rules applicable to the flight allowed the aircraft to be flown as low as 50 feet above ground with a minimum cloud base of 250 feet and minimum visibility of 1 kilometre[36]. IFR required the aircraft to be at least 1000 feet above the highest obstruction *en route* (Q 280). Sir John reckoned that the way point change was made some 20 seconds before impact; and he accepted as facts from the simulation that the groundspeed of the aircraft at the time of height disclosure was 160–175 knots with the aircraft in a cruise climb[37], and that the crew started to flare the aircraft some 4 seconds before impact.

134. In Sir John's view, by continuing a cruise climb towards the Mull after the way point change, when they could have selected a high rate of climb, turned away from the high ground and stayed out of cloud or slowed down and then flown along the coast, the pilots "grossly breached the rules of airmanship" (Q 280). Sir John was clear that the gross negligence occurred at the way point change or a little before but he did not know when. If as he believed the crew voluntarily climbed into cloud, "the moment they decided to climb into cloud and go on to instrument conditions was the moment of negligence, because at that point they needed to take decisive action to make safety altitude as quickly as possible or not to fly any further towards the Mull until they had established that safety altitude" (Q 314).

135. During the course of his evidence Sir John on more than one occasion emphasised that his conclusions were based on fact and not on hypotheses. It is therefore appropriate to look at some of the matters which he treated as fact. (Page references are to HL Paper 25(i).)

(a) "We know that about 20 seconds before impact with the ground the crew made a way point change" (Q 280, p 118 col 1). This figure which derives from the Racal

---

[36] If flying slower than 140 kts indicated airspeed. If faster, 1.5 km. Illustrated on slides 4 and 5.

[37] A cruise climb is a climb at high forward speed and low ROC. To increase ROC, forward speed must be reduced.

report on the SuperTANS is based on a power down speed of 150 knots and a straight course from the WP change to impact at that speed. It is therefore at best an estimate and not a fact since the only factual evidence of speed at or after the change is the indication from the ground speed and drift indicator of 147 knots at initial impact (AAIB report, paragraph 7).

(b) "We know for a fact ... that some four seconds before impact the crew started to flare the aircraft" (Q 280, p 117 col 1; Q 1088). Not so. The Boeing simulation, using assumptions now shown to be incompatible, produced this result. On no view could it be described as fact and there is no evidence either way as to what caused the aircraft to impact the ground in the position described in the AAIB report.

(c) "They had chosen to fly straight over the Mull of Kintyre, and we know that because they had set up this 1000 feet a minute ROC" (Q 301). There is no evidence that they had chosen to overfly the Mull, and indeed the making of the way point change suggests the contrary. Furthermore the 1000 feet a minute ROC derives entirely from the Boeing simulation with all its deficiencies referred to above.

(d) "What is for sure is that they were in a 1000 a minute cruise climb in that last 20 seconds before the final four seconds of flare" (Q 304). This is far from being sure given the deficiencies in the simulation already referred to.

(e) "We know they did not pull emergency power" (Q 311). Sir John later agreed that the impact could have destroyed any evidence of emergency power being pulled (Q 1097).

136. An example of Sir John's reliance on facts appears in the evidence given on his first appearance before us: "The judgment I have made about gross negligence is not based on what I think may have happened, it is based on what I know happened from the facts I have described to you" (Q 321). The majority of these "facts" were the matters referred to in the preceding paragraph.

137. Sir John in his remarks had discounted the possibility of a control jam, saying that the crew flew "a serviceable aircraft" into the hill. On first appearing before us he was asked about the possibility of the crew having lost control of the aircraft due to a control jam; he explained that if this had happened the pilots would have pulled emergency power, which they had not done because the relevant captions had not been activated. He therefore discounted this as a possibility (QQ 310–11). Nevertheless he later said that he could not exclude the possibility of a control jam having played a part in the accident (Q 339); and his acceptance that evidence of emergency power having been pulled could have been destroyed (see para 135(e) above) necessarily weakens his argument against such a jam having taken place. He emphasised however that "the crew put themselves into a position where they were going to hit the mountain and if any subsequent technical failure happened they had forsaken all the margins of safety which are imposed upon our aircraft". Although he could not exclude the possibility that some technical event such as an engine failure caption distracted the pilots, he considered it incomprehensible "that a minor emergency would have so distracted them that they forgot they were about to hit a mountain" (Q 340). Likewise Sir William Wratten conceded that the possibility of a control jam or engine malfunction could not be disproved (Q 1068).

138. On 11 December 2001, some weeks after our last public hearing and when the first draft of our report had been almost completed, we received a document from the MoD entitled "Turning Performance of Chinook" (p 73 of HL Paper 25(ii)). This document stated the position of the MoD and was no doubt intended to support the views of the Air Marshals that the aircraft was already in a position of danger at the way point change. The document set out information about the radius of turn of which a Chinook is capable, in an attempt to show that it was inevitable that if the aircraft had turned at the point of way point change, banking 30 degrees, there would have been a crash. It is

unfortunate that the Air Marshals did not provide us with this information on either of the two occasions on which they gave evidence. The document assumed a fairly high airspeed and did not take account of the possibility that, if the crew had on initiating a turn reduced speed, the radius of turn could have been greatly reduced. The formula for calculating the radius of turn contained in the document was helpful in demonstrating the dramatic effect of a reduction of speed in reducing that radius.

139. On 7 January 2002 we received a further letter from the MoD offering "key information about the speed of ZD 576". This letter stated that at 1747 hrs the aircraft was observed on radar to be about 7 nm on the 27° radial from Belfast VOR. "The crash took place at 1759.30, 35 nm down track, so the aircraft must have maintained average cruising speed in excess of 150 knots groundspeed".

140. If this information was considered to be of crucial importance, we fail to understand why it was not drawn to our attention several months previously. However, we do not consider that it is of such importance. First, while it produces an average speed over the 35 nm, it throws no light on the actual speed at the way point change. Second, even if the speed at the way point change were 150 knots or more, this would not reflect on the pilots' ability to reduce speed on making a turn to port. Third, it adds no support to the Boeing simulation, since 150 knots groundspeed equates in the circumstances to only 125 knots airspeed. Boeing found it impossible to match the predicted conditions with the initial impact data as found when the airspeed at the start of the final manoeuvre was 135 knots or below.

141. Both Sir John and Sir William gave evidence for the second time after we had heard all the other witnesses. Sir John explained that way point A entered in the TANS was in fact some 280 metres south east of the lighthouse. He produced a map (reproduced in HL Paper 25(i), p 157) showing the track of the aircraft to the programmed way point with a mark thereon for the point at which the aircraft would have been one kilometre from the land. He considered that if the crew had intended to fly VFR along the west side of the Mull they should, at the high speed at which they were travelling, have altered course at that point; and that they were negligent in not having done so (Q 1042). Had they turned at the point of way point change which was only 600 metres from the cliffs they would have been in a dangerous position. Had they turned where they thought they were when they made the way point change, namely to the west of the actual track, the cliffs would have been about 1 kilometre ahead (see map) and the change would not have attracted criticism from Sir John and Sir William (Q 1039).

142. Sir William also considered that if the crew were visual with the Mull they should have turned left at 1 kilometre away (Q 355). He stated that if there had been a control jam preventing an alteration of course immediately after the way point change the pilots would have been negligent because "they had brought upon themselves an emergency, a crisis of time" (Q 376).

143. Sir William summed up his position by agreeing with the proposition that the aircraft should not have been in either of the way point change positions (namely that in which they actually were and that in which they thought they were) and that any supervening circumstances affecting the flight at or after reaching these positions were irrelevant (QQ 438–42). In fairness to Sir William it should be explained that these answers were simply agreements to propositions put to him, and should be read together with his answers to QQ 335 and 1039. Both Sir John and Sir William considered that the aircraft must have been under control when the way point was changed and when the final flare was initiated 4 seconds before impact.

PART 6: CONCLUSIONS

144. When they drafted their remarks upon the investigating board's report both Air Marshals had before them evidence as to weather conditions at the lighthouse and higher up the hill, and Mr Holbrook's single answer to the board, from which they deduced that the conditions of cloud prevailing at the lighthouse would have prevented the pilots from seeing the Mull as they approached it.

145. Mr Holbrook's evidence to the FAI and to us puts a different complexion on the matter. We also saw a photograph taken by a Mrs M J Gresswell at the lighthouse minutes before the crash in which the sea appeared to be visible; but this was not altogether clear and it would be unwise to place too much reliance on it. However, in the light of Mr Holbrook's evidence together with the views of Group Captain Crawford that the crew had seen the Mull when they made the way point change and the evidence of Witness A to the same effect, we conclude that the crew had probably seen the land mass at or before the time the way point was changed. Squadron Leader Burke said that he had flown to the Mull and very similar areas and that a line of breakers could nearly always be seen even if nothing else (Q 779). Given an onshore wind of 25 knots (force 6 on the Beaufort scale) it seems more than probable that breakers would be readily visible from a low-flying aircraft out at sea.

146. Negligence, as a concern of the board, was not an abstract concept but could only be inferred from facts relevant to causation. Paragraph 1 of Annex G to Chapter 8 of AP3207 stated that causes of accidents broadly speaking fell into three categories: technical faults, natural operating or medical hazards and human failings. Paragraph 2 provided among other things:

> "Before making a detailed assessment of human failings the board must distinguish between those irregularities which had no direct connection with the cause of the accident and those which had. This can be resolved by the answers to two questions:
>
> a. Was the person's act which is under consideration an essential link without which the final event would not have happened?
>
> b. Ought the person to have foreseen that their action or their failure to take action would in all probability occasion the final event?"

147. In the context of the Air Marshals' conclusion that the pilots were grossly negligent in placing the aircraft in the position in which it was at or before the way point change was made, regardless of what happened thereafter, the question to be answered is *whether there is absolutely no doubt whatsoever that they ought to have foreseen that their action would in all probability occasion the final event*. It must be borne in mind that it is not known at what height or speed the aircraft was flying at the way point change, nor its position in relation to cloud. However Sir William accepted the possibility that they could have seen the coastline under cloud cover (Q 364). Furthermore the Air Marshals' views as to the danger of the aircraft being at or in the vicinity of the way point change position even if the crew had intended to alter course at that point were much influenced by the high speed at which they assumed the aircraft then to be travelling – an assumption which, having regard to the deficiencies in the simulation which have now emerged, may no longer be justified.

148. We consider that Sir John's conclusions on this matter must be weakened by his reliance on matters which he treated as facts but which have been demonstrated to our satisfaction to be not facts but merely hypotheses or assumptions. It must be a matter of speculation what would have been the Air Marshals' conclusion if the Boeing simulation had not been available, or if its deficiencies had been identified.

149. Sir John stated that at the speed at which the aircraft was going the crew would have needed to start a 30 degree bank turn at the point where the way point was changed "if

they were to stand a reasonable chance of not striking the ground". The necessary angle of bank would have increased as the aircraft approached the land (Q 1032). This of course assumes that the aircraft was then and thereafter under control, travelling at the groundspeed of 174 knots (150 knots airspeed plus 24 knots tailwind) used by the Boeing simulation. He further said that if they had left it to the way point change "they probably, possibly, would have hit the cliffs even in the turn" (Q 1042). He later described a turn in such circumstances as "dangerous" (Q 1060). He made no reference however to the possibility that the crew in making such a turn could have reduced speed, thereby significantly reducing the radius of turn, a result well demonstrated by the formula referred to in paragraph 138 above.

150. Sir William appeared to accept that if, having visibility of 1000 metres, the crew had altered course at the way point change and flown maintaining visual contact with the coast, they would have been "perfectly entitled" to do this (QQ 355, 394, 1039). However on his second appearance he rather departed from this view and explained that, if the aircrew had 1000m visibility, they would have seen that they were displaced from their planned track some 8 or 9 seconds before they made the way point change, and should therefore have altered course earlier (Q 1059). Both Air Marshals attached importance to the results of the simulation, and in particular to the high speed at which the aircraft was assumed to be travelling at or before the way point change, an importance which must now be considered doubtful given the deficiencies already referred to in the simulation. In any event, even if the aircraft was travelling at the assumed high speed at or before the way point change, no reason has been suggested as to why speed could not have been reduced in making any subsequent turn, thereby reducing its radius.

151. This evidence certainly does not justify a finding that there is absolutely no doubt whatsoever that an alteration of course at or very shortly after the actual point of way point change would have resulted in a crash. In this context Squadron Leader Burke's view as to the Chinook's ability to spin round "just like a top" (Q 747) must also be taken into account.

152. We have approached the foregoing question upon the basis that the way point change was made when the aircraft was some 600 metres from the cliff. This assumes that the position divulged by the TANS was precisely accurate – an assumption which may not be justified. It will be remembered that the TANS recorded the height above sea level of the point of impact as 665 ft (± 50), whereas in fact it was 810 ft (see above, para 53). If the aircraft had been on the programmed track it would probably have been 1 kilometre from land ahead at the way point change and there is no suggestion that an alteration of course at that point would have resulted in a crash.

153. If as we consider to be the case there was no justification for holding that the pilots were negligent in placing the aircraft at the actual way point change, the next question is whether nevertheless there was evidence which would justify a finding of negligence in relation to subsequent events. If, in the knowledge that they were close to high ground, whether at the assumed or actual way point change, the pilots voluntarily thereafter maintained course and speed until they reached the point where no actions on their part would avoid a crash, then there would be no doubt as to their negligence. Is this what happened?

154. Ever since the final proceedings of the Board were made known there has been much discussion in Parliament, the media and elsewhere as to why two highly skilled helicopter pilots, knowing how close they were to high ground, should have deliberately flown their aircraft into that ground. It has been suggested that this scenario is positively bizarre, particularly in view of the making of the way point change some seconds before.

155. Air Commodore Crawford, in addition to commenting in his Remarks on the significance of the way point change, stated in evidence that it would have been very unwise to have altered the way point if it was intended not to alter course but to fly over the Mull and he did not think that any normal pilot would have done it (Q 872). Witness A was asked whether he could think of any reason why having changed the way point the aircraft should have continued on its existing course at an apparently slow ROC to the Mull. He replied, "That is the crux of the matter. I cannot think of any reason why the crew would have elected to do that unless they were not doing it of their own volition" (Q 802).

156. Witness A later pointed out that the Special Forces crews exercised regularly in the area and that all of the crews were pretty familiar with the landscape and weather conditions associated with it. He continued, "I have operated with both of the individuals concerned in that area a number of times and it would be normal practice, if the visibility was poor, to remain below the cloud level and use the coastline, as we call it, as a 'handrail' and follow the coastline up towards the next turning point. So I can think of no reason why they should commit themselves to instrument flight in that area if they could see the Mull." It was put to him that the finding of negligence was based on the premise that the act of negligence was not changing to IFR 20 seconds or so before impact: was there any reason why they should change to IFR if their visibility was all right? He replied, "Absolutely none, my Lord. Everything pointed towards them continuing VFR flight, both the weather, the task, the icing limitation on the aircraft, everything pointed towards them continuing that flight VFR." He was asked whether the way point change was further evidence pointing in the same direction; he replied that it was (QQ 836–8).

157. Witness A also referred to the quite dramatic down-draughting and turbulence likely to be present on the west side of the Mull with the wind from 170 degrees as another good reason for the crew to turn away early from the land (Q 849). Squadron Leader Burke explained that if a way point was changed the pilot would not normally be expected to maintain the existing course unless he wanted to fly to a point to update the navigation system, something he could not do in bad weather (Q 779).

158. It is clear from the evidence of both Squadron Leader Burke to us (Q 779) and Witness A to the FAI[38] that if the crew had altered course at the way point change they would not necessarily have adopted the course indicated by the TANS but could have perfectly properly altered course further to port and then flown a course to Corran over the sea and parallel to the coast possibly at a reduced height. There is, of course, no evidence that the low cloud hugging the upper part of the Mull extended to any measurable extent over the sea.

159. Against that background the movements of the aircraft after the way point change must be considered. At the risk of repetition it may be worth setting out again such information as could be gathered about the last seconds of the aircraft's flight:

(a) a way point change was made at recorded distances

   (i)   of 0.81 nm from way point A which was not the lighthouse but a position some 280 metres to the south east thereof due to a technical error in the TANS and a fault in programming, and

   (ii) of 0.95 nm from the point of impact,

(b) the TANS recorded the height of the aircraft between 15 and 18 seconds before power down as 468 feet plus or minus 50, and

(c) the initial impact of the aircraft to the ground was at a height of 810 feet above mean sea level.

---

[38] Unpublished transcript, p 2352 C.

160. Initial impact estimations deduced from marks on the ground and the state of the wreckage which were considered by Mr Cable to be reliable (AAIB statement para 6) were:

Flight path –	20 Up relative to the horizontal
Pitch Angle –	30 Nose up approx
Roll Angle –	5–10 Left
Yaw Angle –	Probably less than 10
Track –	025 M(L) [i.e. approx 015 (G), 012 (T)]
Forward groundspeed –	Considerably in excess of 100 knots

161. There is however no evidence to establish (a) the time of the way point change, (b) the height of the aircraft at the way point change, (c) the position of the aircraft when at the recorded height, (d) the course and speed of the aircraft at either of the two foregoing events or indeed at any time prior to impact, nor (e) that the aircraft was in cloud at the time of the height recording. Given the evidence of Mr Holbrook that the cloud was hugging the land, the fact that it was at or below 300 feet at the lighthouse throws no light on conditions prevailing either at the way point change or at the unknown position of the aircraft to seaward some 15 to 18 seconds before impact.

162. The Boeing simulation was prayed in aid to fill in some of the foregoing gaps but as already described it can only determine what could have happened rather than what did happen and was itself deficient in the following respects, namely (i) it did not take account of FADEC, (ii) it postulated a combined speed and ROC which have been found by Witness A and Sir John Day to be unattainable, (iii) it also produced a rotor speed of 91 per cent which was a fairly extreme position differing considerably from that found on the instrument panel and of whose accuracy Mr Cable had doubt, (iv) it produced a groundspeed during the final manoeuvre of 158 knots which exceeded by 11 knots the speed of 147 found in the ground speed indicator, and (v) it hypothesised a final manoeuvre initiated by the crew some 4 seconds before impact, and that prior thereto the aircraft had been under control on a steady course and speed.

163. Both Air Marshals accepted as a matter of fact that the aircraft was under control when the way point change was made and at the moment 4 seconds before impact when the simulation assumed that the final flare was initiated. So far as the way point change is concerned we accept that it is highly unlikely that the crew would have made a way point change if they had thought that they were not in control, but it is possible that if some loose article had jammed the controls during steady flight this would not manifest itself until the controls were moved in order to alter course. Squadron Leader Burke referred to his experience of test flying with control and engine malfunctions when after a period of steady flight dormant faults can appear when a manoeuvre is initiated or engine speed is reduced or increased (Q 705). There is no evidence that such was the case here but equally no evidence that it was not. Alternatively, the movement of the controls to alter course could have precipitated a jam.

164. So far as the aircraft being under control at the moment four seconds before impact is concerned, we do not consider that there is evidence to justify such a conclusion to the required standard of proof. Indeed, apart from the simulation, such evidence as there is – to which reference will shortly be made – suggests the contrary.

165. Both Sir John and Sir William accepted that the possibility of a control jam or engine malfunction could not be disproved. They were adamant however that the pilots were faced with no problem prior to the way point change and that their negligence in reaching that position was not mitigated by anything that might have happened thereafter (QQ 339, 1069–71).

166. If however the finding of negligence at or before the way point change has not been established to the required standard of proof, as we consider to be the case, this proposition does not stand up. The evidence before us was entirely consistent with an intention to alter course and fly VFR to Corran and equally inconsistent with an intention to continue on the same course over the Mull under IFR.

167. The AAIB were not able to exclude the possibility of a control jam given the level of system damage. Nor could they exclude the possibility of pre-impact detachment of the thrust balance spring attachment bracket and other inserts. It will be remembered that this bracket had some three weeks previously detached from the aircraft's thrust/yaw control pallet (see above, para 56). The AAIB were unable to assess the functionality of number 1 DECU owing to gross fire damage. Metallic contamination of the hydraulic system of the integrated lower control actuators found by the AAIB was thought to have been present pre-impact but not to have contributed to the accident; however, the subsequent experience of the US Army and their recommendations (see para 104 above) suggest that such contamination could cause disturbance in the normal operation of those components at the time. DASH runaways have caused temporary loss of control problems as Squadron Leader Burke explained, and UFCMs and false engine failure captions have also afflicted Chinook Mk 2s. Mr Cable accepted that it was possible that there had been an intermittent engine fault which had subsequently reverted to normal before the impact. The problems arising from the newly installed FADEC system had not all been resolved by June 1994; and the Boeing simulation has been shown to have relied to some extent on postulations which are impossible in performance and parameters some of which do not fit with what was found by the AAIB. Can it in these circumstances be said that there is absolutely no doubt whatsoever that it was the voluntary action of the aircrew – including not only both pilots but also MALM Forbes who in our view was probably assisting with the navigation – which caused the aircraft to fly into the hill?

168. Squadron Leader Burke, when asked whether he saw anything significant in the position of the rudder pedals which were at 77 per cent of full travel, replied that it was "an enormous rudder input", unthinkable at high speed (Q 719; see above, para 112). He had also referred to this matter through one of the papers which he had submitted to the Committee in the following terms: "The position of the rudder pedals on impact (almost full left rudder), the high impact speed, and the fully up, or close to fully up, lever position coupled with 100.5% N_R[39] and only 70% torque suggest that an erratic flight path typical of a partial control loss is the most likely of the many guesses as to what was happening in the cloud on ZD 576's last seconds of flight".

169. Witness A commented, "There is absolutely no reason for applying that amount of yaw pedal during forward flight and the only reason I can think of for applying that much yaw pedal would be if the aircraft was becoming extremely difficult to control" (Q 807). He went on to state that the view of the Board that the pedals had been displaced by impact could not be ignored either.

170. Squadron Leader Burke expressed the view that the most likely cause of the accident was a jam of some kind affecting the control of the aircraft, perhaps arising from displaced articles in the broom cupboard (Q 738). A UFCM resulting possibly from a DASH runaway and causing temporary loss of control was also considered by him to be a possibility (Q 739). Such a runaway could cause a temporary increase in rotor speed which the pilot would seek to contain by raising the collective lever thereby forcing the aircraft to climb perhaps unexpectedly into cloud.

171. Witness A considered a control jam to be a strong possibility for the cause of the accident but certainly not an exclusive one (Q 806). He also cited the possibility that a control problem in pitch could have produced oscillations which resulted in the 30

---

[39] Rotor rotational speed.

degrees pitch up position in which the aircraft was found (Q 844). Mr Perks expressed the view in his second memorandum that a major mechanical flight controls failure could be an explanation for the difficulty which Boeing experienced in matching their simulation to the data provided.

172. We consider the evidence of Mr Holbrook as to the probability of the pilots being able to see the lower part of the Mull to be of considerable importance – evidence which unfortunately was not before the Air Marshals when they carried out their reviews. For the reasons already given we do not think that the Boeing simulation merits the status which has been accorded to it in the past, and that even if there were some last minute manoeuvre of the aircraft it cannot be said that there was absolutely no doubt whatsoever that it was initiated by pilots who were in control of the aircraft.

173. It follows that the Air Marshals were not justified in concluding that the pilots were in control 4 seconds before impact, or at any time after the way point change. In short it has not been established to the required standard of proof that it was the voluntary action of the pilots which caused the aircraft to fly into the hill.

174. In carrying out our terms of reference, **we have considered the justification for the Air Marshals' finding of negligence against the pilots of ZD 576 against the applicable standard of proof, which required "absolutely no doubt whatsoever". In the light of all the evidence before us, and having regard to that standard, we unanimously conclude that the reviewing officers were not justified in finding that negligence on the part of the pilots caused the aircraft to crash.**

175. We consider it appropriate to identify those matters to which we have had regard which were not before the Air Marshals when they considered the investigating board's report:

(a) the more detailed evidence of Mr Holbrook as to the weather conditions at sea, and the probability that the crew would have seen the land mass from some distance offshore;

(b) the evidence of Mr Perks, Witness A and Squadron Leader Burke;

(c) the deficiencies in the Boeing simulation with particular reference to the facts that

(i) it did not take account of FADEC and

(ii) it used a postulated speed and ROC which have been shown to be incompatible; and

(d) the possible effect of contamination in the hydraulic fluid in the integrated lower control actuators, as referred to in the US Army report of June 1997.

176. How could it be that a very experienced crew, having planned to fly VFR, having taken when probably visual with the Mull the appropriate steps to alter course, when there was nothing to prevent them flying northwards within sight of the coast, flew into the Mull? It is as Sir John and Sir William speculatively described "incomprehensible" (Q 342) and "astonishing" (Q 377). We shall never know.

APPENDIX 1

Membership

Lord Brennan
Lord Bowness
Lord Hooson
Lord Jauncey of Tullichettle (Chairman)
Lord Tombs

The Committee was given power to appoint Specialist Advisers but chose not to do so.

Lord Tombs declared a relevant interest as an honorary Fellow of the Royal Aeronautical Society.

APPENDIX 2

Witnesses

The following gave oral evidence:

RAF Board of Inquiry

Air Chief Marshal Sir William Wratten GBE CB AFC CIMgt, RAF retd

Air Chief Marshal Sir John Day KCB OBE ADC BSc, RAF

Air Commodore Peter Crawford, RAF retd

Group Captain Andrew Pulford, RAF

Contributors to the RAF Board of Inquiry

Air Accidents Investigation Branch

Mr Mark Holbrook

Squadron Leader David Morgan, RAF

Others

Mr Michael Tapper

Captain John Cook

Squadron Leader Robert Burke, RAF retd

Captain Ron Macdonald FRAeS

Captain Richard Hadlow FRAeS

Captain Ralph Kohn FRAeS

A further witness, identified as Witness A, was granted anonymity

The following supplied written material. In the case of those marked * it is printed in HL Paper 25(ii). In the case of those not so marked, it is available (unless confidential) for inspection in the House of Lords Record Office (020 7219 3074).

Mr Edward Albrecht

Mr S Campbell

Campaign Support

Mr D J Carey

Computer Weekly

Lord Cooke of Islandreagh

Wing Commander J A Cooke OBE, RAF

Mr Thomas Crawford

*Ministry of Defence (selected submissions published only)

Mr R France

Air Chief Marshal Sir Michael Graydon

Mrs M J Gresswell

Mr John Griffin

Mr David Harrison

Mr B Hepburn

Air Commodore D J Hine

Mr Hadrian Jeffs

Air Chief Marshal Sir Richard Johns

Mr A Lawrence

Captain Omar Malik

Mr David Martin

Mr G G Meekums

Mr John Nichol

Mr D E Pedgley

*Mr Malcolm Perks

Mr William Pike

Dr Gordon Pledger

Public Accounts Committee, House of Commons (published in HL Paper 67 2000–01)

Mr J M Ramsden

Mr Michael Russell

Squadron Leader Bernie Smith

Mr Malcolm Spaven

Mr Nevin Taggart

Mr Douglas Tott

Mr David Walmsley

Mr P Weaver

*****

APPENDIX 3

Glossary

A&AEE	Aircraft and Armament Experimental Establishment, Boscombe Down
AAIB	Air Accidents Investigation Branch, an agency of the Department of Transport, Local Government and the Regions
DASH	Differential air speed hold
DECU	Digital engine control unit
FADEC	Full Authority Digital Engine Control
FAI	Fatal Accident Inquiry
IAS	Indicated air speed
IFR	Instrument Flight Rules
ILCA	Integrated lower control actuator
IMC	Instrument Meteorological Conditions
LCTA	Longitudinal cyclic trim actuator
MALM	Master Air Loadmaster
MoD	Ministry of Defence
Q	Question in oral evidence
ROC	Rate of climb
SA	Safety Altitude
TANS	Tactical Area Navigation System
UFCM	Undemanded flying control movement
VFR	Visual Flight Rules
WP	Way point, as programmed in the TANS

Units of measurement

kt	knot (one nautical mile per hour, 1.1515 mph)
nm	nautical mile (1852 metres, 1.1515 miles)

Printed in the United Kingdom by The Stationery Office Limited
2/2002   701787   19585   CRC Supplied

ISBN 0-10-406302-5

9 780104 063026